OLD MONEY AMERICA

Aristocracy in the Age of Obama

JOHN HAZARD FORBES

iUniverse, Inc.
New York   Bloomington

Old Money America
Aristocracy in the Age of Obama

iUniverse books may be ordered through booksellers or by contacting:

iUniverse
1663 Liberty Drive
Bloomington, IN 47403
www.iuniverse.com
1-800-Authors (1-800-288-4677)

ISBN: 978-1-4502-0276-3 (pbk)
ISBN: 978-1-4502-0278-7 (cloth)
ISBN: 978-1-4502-0277-0 (ebk)

Printed in the United States of America

Illustrated by Audrey Heffner-Villegas

iUniverse rev. date: 2/25/2010

Figure 1: Dedication: Here's To You

To Christina Keely Porter Forbes, daughter of Thomas Vandiveer Porter III and Antoinette Benson Porter

From you all, such riches of the heart!

CONTENTS

Figure 2: An Introduction to Old Money

AN INTRODUCTION TO OLD MONEY

The Fundamentals of Old Money

*People are fascinated by the rich: Shakespeare
wrote plays about kings, not beggars.*

—Dominick Dunne

The upper class. The upper crust. The elite. Brahmans, blue bloods, and high society. Patricians, plutocrats, and aristocrats. Each describes Americans who have enjoyed generations of wealth and prestige. Such people never use these terms. Old Money is preferred.

Immediate questions arise. How old is old enough? And how much is money enough? Where are these people? How did they get rich? How do they stay rich? If they are truly something apart, what makes them so?

There are no rigid guidelines. Old enough is more than

three generations in easy circumstances, and money enough is having few worries about life's necessities. Where does Old Money live? This is America, and Old Money is everywhere. While including the legendary rich of Greenwich and Palm Beach, Old Money is found in every town nationwide. Both Park Avenue and Altoona have Old Money.

How did they get rich? Renowned wealth flowed from oil, steel, railroads, and banking; Rockefeller, Carnegie, Vanderbilt, and Morgan were fabled tycoons. Yet most Old Money comes from the ordinary stuff of life. Behind every stove, spot remover, or over-the-counter pill is some lesser-known Old Money family. The formula for all old fortunes is the same: follow a need to its logical conclusion. The famously rich made empires while the quietly rich made long johns.

How does Old Money stay rich? That money marries money is an ancient truism, and multigenerational histories of financial ups and downs can be instructive. If Old Money has one golden rule, it is to hang on to everything forever, including stocks and land. When the 1929 crash hit, middle-class investors sold out at any price; upper-class investors hung on and waited out bad times, eventually enjoying colossal returns. However, there is no magic. Even though patricians imply having almost supernatural financial savvy, most fortunes persist through the simple arithmetic of compounded interest.

The Old Money ethos sits on a tri-legged stool of three

assumptions: wealth, assurance, and prestige. Prestige is the most important. The nouveaux riches have money and confidence but not the prestige that sets the gentry high above. While Old Money cannot be determined by net worth alone, some characteristics are universal. Old Money has strict codes of dress and deportment. Men and women with Old Money live in ageing houses amid stuff that other people don't own or even want. Most ingrained is their speech, a vocabulary of seemingly simple words freighted with nuance. And mind-boggling contradictions reign over everything, contradictions that insiders comprehend and outsiders find mystifying. This is not limited to Anglo-Saxon Protestants.[1] Regardless of race or ethnic origins, established families eventually adopt similar manners, quirks, and preoccupations. Distinguished blacks in Washington are much like genteel Iranians in Pennsylvania and affluent Scots in Florida. All carry the same Old Money consciousness. They are acutely aware of representing and maintaining a high station, while ever wary of loss and embarrassment.

I wrote this book in 2009, a tough time for old assumptions. With the age of Obama come economic, political, and cultural shifts that make everyone feel unmoored. Anybody believing that privileged people float above it all on cloud nine is misguided.[2] Even the most stiff-necked Brahman admits that the wealth, assurance, and prestige of high society are fading. Another question arises: can Old Money's assumptions survive into the twenty-first century?

This book is neither a hymn of praise nor a Marxist rant, and I appreciate the pitfalls of blanket statements about thousands of people. As with any group, from-money people have qualities that are both charming and churlish. My goal is to present reasonably balanced observations about Old Money's characteristics. Then again, the higher tier always treats me as an insider. So here is a caveat within a conundrum: the best people are on their best behavior around each other. As it is impossible for me to be a different person, it is impossible for me to report how other upper-class people behave when not among their own kind.

The information I share is based on my experiences, along with some published corroboration. By the dubious virtues of my name, ancestry, education, and finances, I have a ticket into the Old Money tent. Nevertheless, my attitudes toward Old Money are ambivalent. I both live within that milieu and step out of it as an observer. This is partly from my upbringing. Although born in New York, I spent most of my childhood in Battle Creek, Michigan, where my father was an executive with Kellogg's. While billions of dollars poured from its factories, there was nothing posh about Battle Creek. [3] I grew up amid decent, no-nonsense people from every level. This invaluable experience gave me the ability to regard Old Money with a cool eye. I was also fortunate to be at the University of Pennsylvania during the tenure of Professor E. Digby Baltzell, best known as coiner of the acronym WASP.[4] Whereas most books about rich people have been more about excess than ethos,[5] he studied the upper class as a specific subculture. Although Baltzell himself was a lion of high society, he was also able to observe it dispassionately.[6]

I worked as a fine-arts appraiser for thirty-five years, a career that demanded detached observation. I identified, listed, and valued special items without personal opinions clouding my judgment. This career offered unusual entrée into the houses and lives of other well-to-do people. As an appraiser, I explored entire houses, including the bedrooms, closets, kitchens, maids' rooms, and attics. Some evaluations were immersions into other lives. When appraising for deaths, divorces, and internecine squabbles, my clients often entrusted me with family secrets. These confidences gave me further insights into how distinctive Old Money attitudes are.

Arcane as it appears, Old Money culture does have validity. Old Money instinctively abhors anything that diminishes human dignity. Its members cultivate understatement and self-restraint with a near-religious devotion to civility. They have given incalculable billions to the civic good and lit the flame that makes America the most generous nation on earth. However, I do not believe the tip-tops have given nearly what they have taken. As American aristocracy withers away, the scales will never be balanced.

I have known the least attractive facet of Old Money: entitlement. My wife and I each had a difficult, silver-spoon grandfather. Their sense of entitlement kept them spoiled children and maimed the lives of everyone around them. Coincidently, my wife and I each had self-made men for our other grandfathers. They were forthright, good-hearted gentlemen and far more admired than their snooty counterparts. These contrasts, so close to home, make me of two minds about so-called aristocrats. Other aspects of Old Money life only underscore my ambivalence. There are people so cosseted by wealth and position that their Belgian shoes never touch the ground. They are upper-class agoraphobics, unable to cope with anything or anybody outside of privilege. To outsiders they seem aloof. To me they are asinine and inept. I'd like to give them a swift kick.[7] Then I observe some patroon quietly acting with such kindness and decency that I cannot despair of the entire caste.

Many things mentioned in this book, such as a reference to Kalamazoo, may seem pulled from the air. They are not. My comments allude to situations I have actually known. To avoid betraying confidences, only public figures are cited as points of reference. In fairness, when my not-all-that-distinguished family is used as an illustration, I will say so.

John Hazard Forbes
Naples, Florida

CHAPTER ONE: '37 PACKARD

The Ironies of Old Money

Cui bono? (Who profits?)

—Cicero

I don't remember much about being four, though I remember being cleaned up and admonished before visiting my great-grandfather, always referred to as "The Judge." To visit him was like coming into the presence of Almighty Oz. Even at four years old, I knew he was more than just all-powerful and all-knowing. "The Judge" had money. Old Money. And every member of the family pinned hopes on getting it.

The Rt. Hon. Frederick Henry Hazard, a New York State appellate justice, was born outside of Utica, New York. His grandparents came out from Rhode Island in the 1820s. They built a Greek revival farmhouse and filled it with the old New-

port furniture now so coveted by connoisseurs. Reviewing the ephemera that have survived, they were genteel people. Their old books reveal that the Hazards had intellectual interests and read transcendentalist literature. Lost to history is why this branch of the Hazards left Newport. There are no tales of quarrels or banishments. My great-grandfather had august relations back in Rhode Island. His cousin Frederick made an enormous fortune mining soda ash. Cousin Caroline was president of Wellesley College and the world's greatest collector of original Elizabeth Barrett and Robert Browning manuscripts.[8] That this country lad became a judge was not all that surprising. He set up practice in Utica, married well, and walked to his law offices until he was ninety-two years old.

By the time I visited his house on Genesee Street, he had long retired from the bench. His second wife, Agnes, greeted us at the door. The Hazards considered her a walking, talking faux pas and a step down from my deceased great-grandmother. Great-grandmother's fortune came from the Ten Eycks of Albany; her money and her diamonds were subjects of much tooth sucking. The house made an impression on me. I recall gloomy, silent rooms with Oriental rugs and a hulking clock in the stair hall. The grand old man was ensconced in his study. He sat behind a desk surrounded by tall bookshelves, looking pink and amiable. He was jovial toward me though I was childishly frightened of him. I also remember a navy blue automobile in his garage. This was the 1937 Packard 12 Club Sedan that he glided in from his house to his courtroom. Packards were big, really big, and the fenders were higher than my head.

Shortly after that visit he died. Oh, the whispered conversations, speculations, and schemes about his money. Even I felt the crash of despair when it didn't pan out as hoped. His estate came to fewer than seventy-five thousand dollars, a chunk of money in 1956, nevertheless splintered into so many pieces that it disappointed everybody. Auntie Hazel packed up the Rhode Island antiques while everyone else attended the funeral, plus she got the diamonds. This evoked decades of keening from my mother; I say the race belongs to the swift. And as nobody wanted that humongous Packard, it was given to the kid who mowed the lawn.

I haven't been back to Utica in forty-odd years. I understand that 2102 Genesee Street is converted to a dentist's office. That '37 Packard, in show condition, is now worth twice the sum total of Great-grandpa's entire estate. For all the family's schemes, the lawn boy made off with what, in the long run, was the greatest treasure. I hope he kept it, and I wish him well.

CHAPTER TWO: HIDING IN PLAIN SIGHT

The Who and Where of Old Money

Money is better than poverty, if only for financial reasons.

—Woody Allen

When Old Money is the subject, too much blather surrounds the tycoon clans.[9] Although they have been extremely rich, to focus only on them narrows the breadth of established wealth in the United States. While there are lots of venerable fortunes in New York, Boston, and Chicago, every American town has Old Money. Each area has families that have lived there for decades, families that staked out the land, built the mills, or started the bank. Enclaves of older colonials and Tudors pop up in unlikely places; the mansions in Hickory Corners, Michigan, rival those of Winnetka.

Three groups are passing through those big homes. First is the old guard, now well into their eighties and fading fast. The second generation are middle-aged baby boomers facing retirement. Boomers are parents of the third set, the Internet generation, or I-gens for short. These three stages represent confidence, anxiety, and indifference. While most families follow the same progression, these shifts from exuberance to uncertainty to apathy are dangerous for Old Money's survival. If the indifference of the Internet generation continues, nobody will carry the gentry's culture forward.

The Best and Brightest: The Old Guard

The old guard were born in the 1920s and '30s and inherited money roughly by the '50s and '60s. These people did not just make rain; they *were* rain. The old guard rode the crest of the American century, enjoying limitless opportunities and unshakable confidence.[10] They benefited from every boom and saw their investments double and redouble.[11] It is almost inconceivable how far money once stretched. Ninety thousand dollars in the 1950s bought a fine house,[12] some good antiques,[13] and a Mercedes,[14] with money left over for college tuition.[15] By 2009 standards, these things total nearly two million dollars.

The Old Money elites were also the power, legal, cultural, and fashion elites. It was an oligarchy. Important matters were settled by swapping favors. Influence given held the expectation of equal influence reciprocated. Having once taken a favor, refusing a favor in return was nigh impossible. Such trade-offs built colleges, founded symphonies, and engendered other ventures for the public good. There was a darker side; these favors included advancing dunderheads and worse. Insiders looked the other way. Outsiders had no clout.

Old guard men tended to be brusque and unaffected. The majority served in World War II or Korea. This was a revelatory experience. In the service, privileged men came to appreciate people of courage and character who were outside their usual circle. And while they would never allude to it, they had faced some horrific situations that knocked the prep school snot clean out of them. While old guard males came back from war still socially superior, they were personally humbled.

In America's booming 1950s and '60s, career qualifications were lenient and good things existed for just the taking. Even technical job requirements were lax.[16] Just-smart-enough really was smart enough. A halfway decent education and a helpful connection started old guard men in solid positions. Capable old guarders did succeed, sometimes spectacularly. That they were the best and brightest was a given. As much as pure talent, these achievements were aided by an expanding economy and an all-male hierarchy. One thing was certain: it was no longer acceptable for a rich gentleman to be idle. A man who couldn't talk business, politics, and sports was a drip.

I never knew an old guard man who counted calories, drinks, or cigarettes. Doctors were avoided, and psychiatry was nonsense. These guys lost no sleep over the cost of a canned ham or a Cadillac. Anything these men saw and liked—such as a boat, a painting, or a dog—they bought on the spot, and often to their wife's dismay. If one male epitomized the ideal it was Nelson Rockefeller.[17] He was supremely rich, personally hardy, and he exuded self-confidence. Old guard men were often stubborn and shortsighted; the absolute assurance of their opinions was grating. Most infuriating was the sometimes-expressed view that they were self-made, conveniently forgetting that the playing field was ever tipped their way. However, their word and a handshake were better than any written contract. To charges that these men were stuck in the 1950s, I'd counter that manners and optimism are old-fashioned too.

Old guard women were more sheltered and reserved than their husbands and brothers. Standards of deportment, speech, and dress were paramount. Anything done poorly, said poorly, or worn poorly besmirched their family honor. It was all about keeping up one's side. If there was an ultimate old guard socialite, it was CeeZee (Mrs. Winston F. C.) Guest. Her all-American beauty, sporty clothes, and unpretentious manners made her the loveliest of lovely ladies. Slim Aarons's 1955 photo of her beside a Palm Beach pool is arguably *the* definitive icon of Old Money in America.[18]

Independent means separated Old Money women from other American wives. Often a woman was better off than her husband. This did not damage the husband's pride because these males were accustomed to moneyed mothers and aunts. High-caste ladies had absolute control over their wardrobes and households; asking their husband's opinion was only a matter of form. Ideally, a couple would share interests, such as golf or gardening or collecting. Certainly anything pertaining to their children was of mutual concern. Yet how bills were paid was fluid from family to family. Two rules were absolute: a gentleman always paid for his clothes, and no lady ever bought herself jewelry or furs.

Few former debutantes held salaried jobs. Instead, charitable projects absorbed a lot of their time. They did not possess a common touch; clubwomen, also called "ladies who lunch," had a reputation for being stuffy. The Junior League combined benevolence with chic, though my family scoffed at do-gooders in Chanel suits. Nevertheless, these women took upon themselves soup kitchens, hospitals, schools, museums, and parks. Prior to the 1970s, government was not much involved in social welfare; public health, arts, and recreation were Old Money's purview. If charities were run like private clubs, they were successful clubs. Such efforts gave ladies who lunched a sense of responsibility, accomplishment, and self-respect.

The old guard's world is passing away as quickly as the old guard itself. Their stubborn refusal to acknowledge change has isolated the old guard and reduced Old Money's authority. In the age of Obama, shortstops make salaries larger than fortunes accumulated over two centuries. The civic good is provided by enormous bureaucracies, and patricians are no longer arbiters of art, fashion, and style. In *Who Killed Society?* author Cleveland Amory answered his own question: the rise of celebrity worship stole the spotlight from Old Money.[19] However, the old guard dies still believing that they kept up their side.

The Dazed and Confused:
The Old Money Baby Boomers

Old Money baby boomers are a new lost generation. Born roughly between the late 1940s and early 1960s, their old guard parents lived so well and succeeded so consistently that it appeared effortless. Well-off boomers had great expectations; they assumed they would ease into lives of power and prestige, then pick up when and where their parents left off. These assumptions proved to be largely false, as Old Money boomers were unprepared for the upheavals of the '60s and beyond. Today, with their expectations dashed, most old-family boomers wonder what went so terribly wrong. There are a marginal few who sail in the same serene waters as their parents; one cannot begrudge that some rich boomers are remarkably smart and able to spin new gold. This tiny minority grabbed the brass ring that most Richie Rich boomers missed.

No old guarder was entirely sheltered from the exigencies of the Great Depression or World War II. Practicality informed their choices. Their boomer children did not feel these constraints. Treading their fathers' footsteps into law, manufacturing, or Wall Street was one possibility, although more intriguing things beckoned in the '60s and '70s. For boomers, to follow one's bliss became a mantra. Even the ultimate boomer went adrift: John Kennedy eschewed politics to play magazine editor, tabloid star, and amateur pilot. Though his story is particularly tragic, it illustrates many of his ilk.[20] True, middle-class boomers also heard these calls to so-called fulfillment. Luckily for them, they lacked great expectations. Most eventually landed in safe jobs and were content to live better than their parents had.

Those from-money boomers who did seek traditional careers rarely found dazzling success. In a nation that increasingly demanded diversity, the old order lost its stranglehold on law, medicine, and finance. Being just smart enough was no longer smart enough, and good things no longer existed for the taking. Top-drawer boomers found themselves in third-drawer jobs. Keeping up appearances became a charade; the big house, private schools, and club dues were ruinous. Other burrs under the saddle were old guard parents. Myopically, the old guard took power and success for granted, and their expectations often edged on the insane. A young father with three kids and just hanging on might find himself criticized for not being in the Senate.

In the early 1980s, just as well-heeled boomers were making career toeholds, the landscape of wealth changed.[21] Astonishing riches came to corporate raiders who played by new rules that the establishment class loathed. For gracious people, the ethics of hostile takeovers, junk bonds, and greenmail were beyond the pale. To their credit, few members of the old regime jumped onto the new frenzy. To their discredit, they took no hard stand against the madness. As people they considered hopelessly crass bounded ahead, patricians did little more than harrumph. Old Money squandered an opportunity to exert leadership. Born-wealthy boomers neither enriched themselves from the change in corporate mores nor enhanced their prestige by demanding openness and fair play.

Worse, as Old Money professionals neared retirement their milieu went ass-over-teapot. The upheavals of 2008–2009 stunned us all. Former gilt-edged securities tanked and white-shoe careers abruptly ended. Scions saw their inheritances wither. Blue-blood professionals feel they have dedicated their lives to jobs they did not like, for security they did not secure, while hoping to obtain what they could never afford. Although middle and working-class boomers also suffered from the 2008 debacle, they were not raised believing an inheritance and a pedigree would see them through.

Those boomers who chose hobby careers flew high for a while. In the 1970s and '80, they set up as horse breeders, gallery directors, or any number of pursuits that had been only recreations for their parents. When times were good these endeavors made profits and were part of an expanding economy. Nevertheless, hobby jobs are contrary to the laws of making fortunes. Old wealth grew from providing practical things to mass markets. Providing specialty things to niche markets has significantly less gravitas. With the 2008–2009 crash, luxury ventures suddenly look like fluff. As their charming shops or spiffy offices are closing, former hobby careerists are at loose ends. At least the hobby careerists attempted something; there were plenty of rich-kid hippies who never even pretended to have careers. They have financed ashrams, trekked Asia, followed every micro-macro-lacto-vegan-bionic diet, and were prey for scammers. Ever adrift, Old Money stoners continue to wander in sunny climes, ponytailed, looking as wrinkly as Ramses and wearing kilos of Navajo jewelry.

My appraiser work was a hobby career, though I did not plan to be self-employed. I walked out of college into the massive 1974 recession and cooked up the appraisal business from desperate necessity. I loved that work. However, forces were against me. All my best clients were born in the 1920s and '30s, or even earlier. As they died off, so did my business. After years of diminishing returns, I abandoned the appraisal business for a job as a foundation director. I am content, not that I had such great success, only that I made no fatal mistakes. A glass half full *is* the new great success, considering how many of my fellow boomers have no glass left at all.

Boomer George W. Bush played at a hobby career, baseball, and then switched to his family's line of work. His success was spectacular or disastrous, depending on one's viewpoint. The quintessential Old Money guys, both Presidents Bush epitomized the wealth, education, loyalty, and stubborn optimism of the old ruling class, even as they pulled off the amazing trick of appealing to the public as good ole boys. Some high muckety-mucks saw this as class betrayal. Worse was George W. Bush's damage to Old Money's prestige. He killed the idea that well-bred men are the white knights of American politics.[22] Bush was hardly alone. Other preppy boys, including Gore, Kerry, and Mc-Cain, acted with equal buffoonery.[23]

Old Money boomers were born on third base during the flush of post-WWII America. They believed that life was an easy jog to home plate. Rare is the from-money boomer who has held on at third base, let alone scored runs. Most are moving backward, toward first base, or entirely out of the ballpark. Their wealth, confidence, and mystique have dwindled. About all they have now is the disconnection be-tween how it really is from how it ought to have been. I join other clear-eyed boomers who acknowledge that for our generation, the best and brightest arose from the middle class. Even the finest and most hardworking blue bloods were just runner-ups.

The Doubtful and Disconnected: The Old Money Internet Generation

I-gens are young adults whose universe is Internet-focused. As cultural identifiers cannot be transmitted via the Web, Old Money speech, manners, and customs have no currency in high-tech America. This leaves kids from manner-born families in a muddle. Among modern youth, upper-class attitudes and behaviors bring reactions of blank incomprehension or outright hostility. Old Money I-gens find themselves isolated and would prefer to drop the whole issue of caste.

As refined society loses its impact on general society, the Internet generation thinks it is ridiculous, if they think of it at all. Old Money youth cannot identify with the triad of wealth, assurance, and prestige. Social deference is absurd to them. They know that the new billionaires make old fortunes look paltry and that nobody has much interest in the quaint niceties of genteel life. Ancestral chattels of antiques, silver, and jewelry are deemed useless. If young Americans can respect and appreciate varying traditions, they can respect and appreciate Old Money culture. To survive, Old Money must bring its best values forward and leave the entitlement and posturing behind. [24] Otherwise, Old Money will become an historical curio.

In 1960, E. Digby Baltzell predicted only two possible fates for the highest echelon.[25] First: it could wall itself within its wealth and allow in nobody new. By doing this Old Money would forfeit leadership yet continue to live in splendor. Or second: American royalty could open itself to new people of achievement and thus retain its dominance. Baltzell failed to envision a third fate: the old establishment would sputter out. He never imagined an upper class that ran short of money, became assured of nothing, and as a group enjoyed less prestige than the fourth lead on a cancelled sitcom. For all of Baltzell's dispassionate observation he was too deeply immersed in his Mandarin existence to hear the distant rumbling. Like the aristocrats of Rome, France, and Russia, he just didn't see it coming.

CHAPTER THREE: HUSH, MONEY

The Financial Secrets of Old Money

Never talk about money.

—Edith Wharton, *A Backward Glance*

Envision a "reading of the will" scene in an old movie.[26] A classy family is ensconced in a paneled library, the men in tuxedos and the ladies in spangled gowns, with a butler hovering nearby. Family members discuss trust funds, bank shares, and oil wells. The clan lawyer arrives, and he recites the terms of a will, proclaiming the net worth of everyone present. Though this can be a handy plot device, it is absolute rot. Gracious families would rather gather at Chick-fil-A to swap pornography than talk about money.

No subject is more taboo among Old Money than money itself. Superior people like to believe that they judge others on manners, not money. This reticence runs deep and reflects many urbane preoccupations, including privacy and decorum. Polite people do not natter about investments, and it is louche to discuss money deals on the golf course. Abhorrence about discussing finances leaves family members uncertain regarding each other's circumstances. Even a spouse's wherewithal may remain hazy, as I can attest. I never ask my wife about her money; it just isn't done. Silence is also a subterfuge for both the richest and least rich. As they are loath to be imposed upon, the ultra wealthy can rest assured that their wherewithal will never arise in conversation. For the less fortunate the pressure to maintain one's station may be at odds with one's bank balance. That the subject of assets is verboten comes as a relief for those who are on their uppers.

The greatest reason for never discussing money is mystique. Grand Pooh-Bahs want to maintain the myth of having secret money knowledge. Passed from generation to generation, this Gnostic wisdom is for certain people to know and lesser mortals to be awed by. Absolute silence about money perpetuates fables of hush-hush investments garnering fabulous returns. This is rubbish. There is no secret money knowledge. Behind all the veils of illusion, Old Money is as exposed to the realpolitik of financial markets as anyone else. In the down sweep of 2008–2009, Old Money has no more places to hide than the average 401(k) investor.

The strategies that have kept the wealthy wealthy are only common sense. One Old Money tenet is to avoid debt, but any smart person knows this. Nabobs are fanatically reluctant to spend on things of no long-term value, resulting in the common notion that rich people can be cheap. The obvious truth here is that saving beats spending. And many dowagers keep all their money in tax-free bonds and high-yield utilities, believing this ploy is uniquely aristocratic. Millions of people seeking security and income do exactly the same. There is the issue of trust funds. Few things inspire such an admixture of awe and ire as trust funds. Although thousands of middle-class people use them for tax savings, trust funds are generally perceived as elitist. The very term is synonymous with entitlement, evoking lives of pampered vacuity. On the contrary, trust funds are much like buckteeth: they are more fun to cogitate about than actually have.

The basic concept of a trust fund is to help the helpless. Assets are set aside to support a person too young, ill, or otherwise unable to manage his or her affairs. Via a legal document, the grantor places money or other property with a trustee. Restrictions on how funds may be used are included in the document. Once signed the wording of a trust cannot be altered. It is the duty of the trustee to see that the bounty is expended for the well-being of the beneficiary. A trust fund has tax advantages over making an outright gift, and, unlike wills, trusts do not become public records.

However, so many elements compose a sizable trust, controlled by so many people with varied agenda and stretching over so many years that trusts often turn counterintuitive. Fortune makers are not foretune tellers, and the original vision of the grantor frequently has no semblance to the reality of the beneficiary. Trusts set up for a child may include restrictions that make the benefits useless to that child when he reaches adulthood. Extensive provisions may be made for future generations that are never born, or specific exclusions for step children and adopted children that grow up to be dearly loved. Attorney, broker, bank, and trustee fees devour the principle. Over time, assets can turn into liabilities: my mother-in-law was saddled with part ownership of an abandoned cemetery, and it cost her thousands to get rid of it. My wife and I will not be setting up any trusts for our granddaughter. We have no desire to make her future complicated and maddening.

If Old Money has enjoyed one huge advantage, it is time. The well-to-do had money when a little money went a really, really long way. For generations, descendants bobbed along nicely not by impenetrable mysteries, but only on the simple arithmetic of time plus interest and dividends, squared. The real secret behind Old Money is that, secretly, there is no secret at all.

CHAPTER FOUR:
THE IVY CHARITY GALA REGISTER

The Three Hallmarks of Old Money

Prestige, *Definition: standing or estimation in the eyes of people. Etymology: from Latin praestigiae, plural, "conjurors' tricks"; from Middle French "illusion."*

—*Merriam-Webster Online Dictionary*

The Ivy League. Charity galas. The *Social Register.* They are the hallmarks of Old Money ascendancy. All denote divine, snotty splendor. Oh, to pass into those promised lands, to blithely step across the divide that separates the aristocratic *we* from the plebeian *them.* It is my sad mission to demystify these three institutions, at least sad for aspiring social climbers. Each is misunderstood, although all are typical of the upper class's mania to preserve their prestige, by wile if necessary.

The Ivy League

I graduated from the Ivy League, the University of Pennsylvania, '74. I have a cousin and a nephew who also went to Penn, and a brother-in-law who taught at Wharton.

In the spirit of full disclosure, I was accepted to a number of excellent colleges, none of which I'd be able to enter today. Thirty-plus years ago, perfect board scores, a 4.0 grade average, and victim status were not requisite for admittance. Still, standards were stiffer in 1970 than in 1918, when my grandfather went to Dartmouth. Rather than make a formal application, he just sent Dartmouth a note that they should expect him in the fall.

While Old Money preens over Ivy League connections, theirs is the nostalgia of "Boola Boola," white flannels, and straw boaters. Anyone who has actually been in the Ivies knows this is bunk. I found Penn down-to-earth. The guys were friendly, unaffected, and nobody worried about financial status. That somebody was very rich or very poor was not a topic of conversation. It was college, not a credit bureau. What snobbery I saw at Penn was limited to a couple of snotty, rich-kid fraternities. The hoity-toity frat boys were easy to spot: they had flippy-floppy hair, chain-smoked, and acted so, so bored. They wore the standard Old Money uniform: Lacoste shirts, rumpled chinos, and deplorable loafers. If they were determined to be inconspicuous they certainly succeeded. Nobody gave them the slightest heed. Yet even these ducks never clomped around in polo togs or white tie, nor did they speak through clenched jaws. The Hollywood version of Ivy Leaguers is just more drivel.

What confuses the masses is that a superior university is about education, not transformation. Professors are not fairy godmothers; the Ivy League does not remodel young people into gentlemen or debutantes. The person who graduates as a senior is the same person who entered as a freshman. Nor does the Ivy League magically turn students into masters of the universe. Perusing the Class Notes of any Ivy alumni magazine reveals careers that, while respectable, are not stupendous. What the best schools offer is an excellent education with wonderful instructors in a first-rate atmosphere. Guarantees of heady accomplishments and social triumphs are not included with each diploma.

Charity Galas

That someone can be awed by charity galas is amazing to anybody who has ever been to one. These gigs are deadly, attended solely out of obligation and the call to keep up one's side. I worked in New York as a foundation director, and I know the charity circuit. Perhaps the sole benefit of a bad economy is that many balls, dinners, teas, tours, and croquet matches are cancelled.

The homely truth behind all the couture and cummerbunds is that special events are pay-to-play rackets. Inclusion is determined by dollars, not doyennes. Anyone who makes a fat enough donation automatically gets invited. Indeed, buying their way onto invitation lists is the first step of all determined social climbers. Invitees purchase tickets to events; after the expenses of food, flowers, and falderol, the net goes to some charity. Actually, it is harder to get hot movie tickets than places at so-called exclusive galas; dozens of seats always go begging. With tickets, even Ralph and Alice Kramden can play swells for a night.

Dismaying as it is, almost nobody at a charity gala feigns much interest in the organization it supports. And the beneficiaries of the largesse are nowhere in sight.[27] Being on a philanthropy board is an Old Money requirement, and only a cynic would mention that board membership is bestowed for the biggest check, not the biggest heart. It is the obligation of everyone within a social circle to attend each other's events. This is the same in New York, Naples, or Kalamazoo. Guests arrive with wooden smiles, make bland chit-chat, pick at mediocre food, and doze through the presentations, always discreetly checking their watches. Some ladies still get a kick from these gigs while most men would rather be in hell hacking off their toes with a chisel. Still, one must keep up one's side.

The *Social Register*

The *Social Register*[28] is a perfect example of Old Money contradiction. This black and orange book is, and then again is not, an address book of America's loftiest people. Every high-toned family is anxious to be included, except all those who want nothing to do with it. Listing implies superior lineage, if one ignores the politicians and CEOs whose lineage is, at best, undistinguished. It is certainly not just a phone book, though it is little else. The *Social Register*[29] is obtainable only by those deemed worthy of inclusion, overlooking the fact that anybody can buy a copy on Amazon.com. One thing is certain: all the confusion surrounding the *Social Register* helps snobs maintain the illusion of prestige.[30]

The *Social Register* is often compared with *Burke's Peerage*.[31] They are not alike. *Burke's* lists all the titled persons of Great Britain and Ireland and names them whether they like it or not. Every title includes genealogical facts. And while the British publication covers more than a million names, nobody in *Burke's Peerage* is beholden to buy a book, pay a fee, or reveal their telephone number. No family breaks into *Burke's Peerage* that is not raised to nobility by the sovereign. The *Social Register* includes only those persons who choose to be listed and has no right to enter any sahib who opts out. Genealogy is not included though phone numbers are. Every household recorded is required to buy two books for an annual cost of about one hundred dollars. Roughly thirty thousand families are involved. And with letters of recommendation, outsiders can break in.

Despite the wealth of the participants, the *Social Register* itself is struggling. Once there were many *Social Registers*, one each for several cities. In the 1970s, costs pressured the publisher to compact all the individual references into one national book. For the uproar, it might have been the fall of civilization; Bostonians were horrified to be listed with Chicagoans. Even in consolidated form the publication continues to lose money. In the age of Obama, the younger generation is not intrigued with the *Social Register*. Its future is anybody's guess.

In the spirit of disclosure, my family was listed in the first *Social Register*, published when Grover Cleveland was president.[32] As far as I am concerned, every family added since then can bugger off. No, I am not listed. The point of it eludes me.

Figure 3: Nuthatch Lane

CHAPTER FIVE: NUTHATCH LANE

The Care and Housing of Old Money

*The rich never apologize for the shabbiness
of their surroundings.*

—Cathy Crimmins

G rey Gardens is an 1890s Shingle-style house in East Hampton. For fifty years it was home to the mother-daughter team of Edith Bouvier Beale and Little Edie Beale. The Beale family was certified Old Money; Jacqueline Kennedy Onassis was kin. The house declined with the Beale fortune, and the two women became the Miss Havishams of postwar America.[33] Although the Beale ladies were exceptionally loony, anybody who has visited Old Money dwellings understands that the context of Grey Gardens was hardly unique. Old Money households lead to one conclusion: these people are crazy.

Like their wardrobes, Old Money homes are never trendy. This was not always true. Early photographs indicate that magnates' interiors were not much different from those of the merely prosperous except in size and gaudiness.[34] Closer inspection may reveal some decent landscapes; however, these often shared wall space with the heads of stuffed critters. During the mid-nineteenth century, rich folks had the means to acquire masterpieces cheaply; Impressionist pictures were inexpensive and eighteenth-century furnishings sold in secondhand shops.[35] Few Victorians had the artistic insight to scoop up such treasures. On matters of household taste, America's most conspicuous consumers had only cubic volume separating themselves from the bourgeoisie.

By 1900 the upper echelon was split between the heirs of founding fathers and the heirs of foundry founders. The colonial faction held the high ground. It stood firm in Federal-era homes, furnished with ancestral chattels. If historic families stayed in creaky houses out of pride or parsimony is debatable. In either case, the more the post-Civil War rich spent the less the pre-Civil War rich loved them. Super-snob Henry James raked the palace builders over in 1908. He deemed their mansions "white elephants" and "really grotesque, while their averted owners, roused from a witless dream, wonder what in the world is to be done with them."[36] Unable to bear the snubs, new money moguls capitulated. They left their curlicue mansions for staid houses of English and American colonial designs. These have remained the favored styles for over a century.

Regal living toned down in style, not in substance. Those decorous Georgian arks were elaborately simple: nothing gaudy, just umpteen rooms needing a phalanx of servants. During their heyday in the 1950s, '60s, and '70s the old guard kept their homes in immaculate splendor. Back then all the best people had more money to spend, lower wages to pay, and more help available for hire. By the 1980s even the old guard quailed at the cost of keeping up big properties. Today the merely well-off cannot bail fast enough. Stuck in a perfect storm of lowered expectations, rising expenses, and the pressure to keep up appearances, most no-longer-flush baby boomers are scrambling to maintain their dowdy-dowager houses. For us, Edgar Allan Poe's *The Fall of the House of Usher* is not a horror story, only the tale of an old family that got behind on repairs.

Old Money districts are remarkably quiet, even in big cities. More than the imposing architecture and mature trees, silence is what makes these neighborhoods true enclaves. Indeed, when a once-grand district becomes noisy, it is the surest sign that the top ranks have moved elsewhere. Regardless of their quiet and wow appeal, rational people admire but do not want Old Money properties. Even the best preserved houses are obviously money pits and wheeze bags to heat, plus the taxes are outrageous. Too many rooms, outdated kitchens, and murky corridors have no general appeal. Only prestige-driven holdouts choose stateliness over economy and convenience.

From the sidewalk, Old Money houses send mixed messages. They are kept up, although not manicured, and minor imperfections are evident. The trim is often peeling while the lawn is shaggy and the bushes need cutting back. This slight disorder carries contradictory information. A visitor senses both an oligarch's disregard for trifling matters and the whisper of downwardly spiraling finances. Insiders understand shabby gentility. Outsiders are mystified that bigwigs seem so careless. People living in demanding properties know that little fixes are like pulling a string on a sweater, and a peeling windowsill can snowball into a new roof. Repairs are put off until disaster strikes and often ignored even then.

Old Money interiors have traits that are perplexing. Disappointment is the common reaction when middle-class people enter upper-class houses. Anybody expecting glittering surfaces, elegant furniture, and brilliant paintings is confounded. More likely a visitor is confronted with disheveled rooms that mix posh with pitiful. Wall colors are dull, painted either pale yellow, pale green, or pale blue. Wallpapers are faded, and the white woodwork has toned to creamy gray. There is too much of everything in a mishmash of traditional styles, and each flat surface is smothered in bric-a-brac. Window and upholstery fabrics are superior quality although limp, and the rugs are shot.

Over everything hovers a distinct Old Money smell: the acrid aroma of wood smoke, big dogs, and stinky English boxwood bushes. The overall effect is not as nonchalant as it appears. This seeming disarray is carefully calculated to signify blue-blood occupants.

A typical front hall has stairs straight ahead with an open arch to the sitting room at the left or right. Opposite the stairs is a mirror over a flip-top table. An antique Chinese umbrella pot is de rigueur as are Oriental runners, a tall-case clock, and bland framed prints. It makes little difference if these items are museum quality or not because the effect is always the same. The sitting rooms, never called living rooms, would be pretty were they not so drained looking. Chairs and sofas are deflated with chintz covers that are askew. Cigarette burns and rings left by wet glasses mar the antique tables. Lamp shades are discolored and at least one objet d'art is poorly mended. These spaces resemble John Koch paintings except the elegant partygoers have vanished.[37] Yet the owners celebrate these weary rooms as indications of ruling-class ennui and aristocratic indifference to petty housekeeping. Again, the message is conflicted: the owners seem unable to afford the bright, fresh interiors that they so distain.

Old Money dining rooms look like corporate boardrooms. There is always a long mahogany table with matching chairs and the inevitable sideboard. A crystal chandelier and big silver tea set are mandatory. The libraries, too, are pro forma: walnut paneling, Persian rugs, leather club chairs, and sporting pictures, though credit must be given for lots of good books. All these rooms are dead still. Nobody sits in the sitting rooms, dines in the dining rooms, or studies in the studies. These are set pieces existing only for prestige value.

Jammed in grandees' homes is stuff that signals only to others of equal rank. If these items are admired for themselves or their status weight is moot. The most desirable decorations are family portraits. That the people depicted may be absolute trolls is beside the point. Like everything inherited, portraits announce that "We are because we were." Clusters of formal photos in silver frames tell the same story. Beat-up furniture is at every turn, many pieces skirting the line between antique and junk; if a masterpiece highboy or wing chair is present, it is likely to be stuck in a gloomy corner. Also prized are heirloom trophies, especially horsey stuff, though yachting cups are supremely classy. The *Town & Country* set has desk and barware from Asprey, Mark Cross, and Cartier; pretty but useless items from Georg Jensen and Steuben add to the ambiance. Chinese export porcelains are highly admired as are, inexplicably, lumpy Staffordshire figures. Social climbers beware: the best people are never fooled by pretenders who purchase heritage items on eBay; the top tier has a sixth sense about such things.

Big old houses have a pantry between the dining room

and the kitchen. The dishes, silver, glassware, and linens kept there are beautiful, even if so impractical as to be downright stupid. The contradictory desire to keep it and get rid of it all stymies the owners. Old Money kitchens are ghastly. These areas need more than just updating; they need the Army Corp of Engineers. Dingy cupboards, chipped sinks, filthy exhaust fans, and worn-out linoleum floors predominate. Gentlefolk affect that kitchens are the help's domain, so they pretend that service areas are beneath notice. No wonder most home buyers take one look and flee.

Vacant servants' quarters underscore the demise of regal living. At her death in 1954, thirty men attended Ruth Twombly's orchids.[38] Style on this scale has disappeared in the United States. The ultra-rich still have help, although few servants live in anymore. We who are merely well-off get by with a cleaning woman. The single truest aristocrat I know carpools her girls, washes dishes, and is familiar with the business end of a vacuum cleaner. Like everybody with useless servants' rooms, she wishes they'd be magically sawed off and pushed into the ocean.

All grand places have converted sunrooms or porches toward the rear. There the TV sits with serviceable chairs and tables. The lords of the realm squash themselves into these regions, hovering near space heaters and eating on card tables. Scions camp out in the back quarters, ever preserving the grandeur of the front rooms. While living with familiar objects is harmless, living *for* these things is questionable. The symbolic value of every chair and teacup outweighs the purpose of each item itself. I am not above this nuttiness. Although I dislike candles, I own thirty-four candleholders, and I waste hours fussing with vintage clocks and watches that don't keep time worth a damn. To paraphrase St. Paul, I am a chief among sinners.

Still, the sum of Old Money interiors outweighs the parts. Only nobility smashes cigarettes in Wan-li dishes, uses Hester Bateman cream jugs as pencil cups, and stacks telephone books on Townsend-Goddard lowboys. No decorator is able to supply aged furniture and faded fabrics to quite the same effect. Layers of family associations cannot be faked while the knitting together of items by time cannot be imitated.[39] And ridiculous as it seems, the ghostly presence of the old cocktail crowd is charming.

As Old Money dies off, only places in superlative locales will survive. The future of gorgeous mansions in rust belt cities is bleak; Detroit already has elegant slums. Any hopes that big properties might become rest homes or conference centers are pipe dreams. Few of these joints would comply with twenty-first-century codes. Like the *Titanic's* Captain Smith, from-money boomers will go down with their ships. Throwing it all over would be too painful, too final a gesture of class betrayal and personal defeat. Wealth, assurance, and prestige cannot reign in a dinky condo. When an aristocrat leaves the manor he leaves the haut monde forever.

WASPs do not have the patent on being house-proud. Anybody believing that there are no snooty African American districts should look deeper.[40] Rich black, Jewish, and other groups have enjoyed exclusive enclaves. Oak Bluffs on Martha's Vineyard, parts of Sag Harbor, and Highland Beach, Maryland, have long been retreats for certain African Americans.[41] Originally created because of religious or racial separations, these areas are desirable in their own right. Many such neighborhoods maintain their ethic unity by selling properties only through word of mouth. This may or may not be a triumph for diversity.

Even the Obamas have fallen into a money pit. They own a Georgian behemoth in Chicago. Because of its historical interest it is unlikely to fall into shambles, although Malia's grandchildren might be reduced to living on the third floor, charging admission, and shifting pots to catch leaks. Old houses do that to people; members of the original family maintain an apartment within The Breakers, the biggest of the big white elephants in Newport. They hole up in a third-floor apartment carved from servants' quarters and try to ignore the hoards of tourists who wander below.[42] For now, the Internet generation is okay with a mattress and anyplace having Wi-Fi. Hercules was tricked by Atlas into taking the burden of the world on his shoulders; I-gens will not be so fooled. They will not exhaust themselves with impossible houses. Mansions will be broken into condo units, abandoned, or demolished. The dynastic furniture, bibelots, and paintings will be off-loaded with no regrets.

When Jacqueline Onassis finally came to aid her desperate relations, only three of twenty-eight rooms at Grey Gardens were habitable.[43] In spite of that, Jackie O. did not help Big and Little Edie leave. She paid for nominal repairs so that they stayed. Logic would have decreed that the property be sold and the women placed in a clean, manageable apartment somewhere. For Old Money that was unthinkable. Better to live amid the feces of feral cats and raccoons than to give up the Hamptons. And better to devolve into mental illness than to live among the middle class. For elites, insouciance and insanity run on the same rails.

CHAPTER SIX: OLD MONEY SPEECH

The Secret Language of Old Money

We are not amused.

—Queen Victoria

During World War II the precursor of the CIA created a special unit of spies. The sons of German American immigrants were recruited to operate deep within Axis territory. Young men were sought who were raised in German-speaking houses within communities having Germanic traditions. After espionage training, small groups were infiltrated into Berlin and other cities. The program was a tragic failure. Not one German American agent survived; all were detected, captured, and shot.[44] Despite their perfect Aryan looks and fluency in the language, some tiny detail always gave them away.

So it is with any group. Even the most studious outsider can never quite pass as a native. It is the same within Old Money ranks. While clothing, conduct, and commonly held experiences denote caste, word choices are the greatest indicator of a certain upbringing. Old Money speech is particularly tricky. The entire high-hat culture is based on the contradiction of being conspicuously inconspicuous. Old Money uses plain words unemotionally delivered in flat tones. Yet those simple, inconspicuous words are loaded with nuance. These are a Morse code to insiders. Outsiders are fools to believe Old Money speaks at face value.

Take the word "nice" as an example. For most people it is a simple word with an obvious meaning. To Old Money it is a code word meaning "unbearable." Add to that adjective the modifier "perfectly" and it is a snob's hand grenade. "Perfectly nice" or "perfectly all right" means just the opposite. Because Old Money thrives on exceptions to any rule, "perfectly lovely" and "perfectly beautiful" are supreme accolades. And watch out: "not nice" expresses far more than a mild disapproval; it is total damnation. Osama bin Laden, for instance, is "not nice."

Many clichés of silver-spoon speech are actually clinkers. No true Newporter affects to say "cottages" in reference to seaside palaces. Rich gentlemen are too polite to say, "If you have to ask, you can't afford it." Upper-class socialites say neither "upper class" nor "socialite." And declaring somebody "NOC," meaning "not our class," is passé. Most of the pompous, snotty phrases used by rich characters in movies and on TV are off base.

Old Money chatter is guarded and rarely more than an exchange of neutral observations. Old Money people avoid frequent use of "I" or "you"; the first seems intrusive and the second inquisitive. The common middle-class conversation starter "What do you do?" is prying and vulgar. Bless them, no polite person digs for free professional advice from any doctor, lawyer, or art appraiser, nor will a gracious individual drone on about his or her ailments. And as within a Masonic lodge, the subjects of politics and religion are shunned.[45] This ability to avoid voicing any personal information is an art form; with positions to maintain and assets to protect the best people feel it necessary to avoid any exposure. Those to the manner-born know that openness leads to chagrin whereas reserve bears no regrets. Safe topics include gardening chatter, favorite old movies, and foods eaten as a child. Same as anybody, Old Money folks love talking about their pets, especially dogs. Many friendships have started not via the drawing room, but by way of the kennel.

The gentry's finest trait is civility. For this reason alone Old Money deserves a place in our ever-ruder world. Nonetheless, politeness has a doppelgänger: exploitation. Being rich and polite often has the same effect as being young and beautiful. Masters of finesse nudge dupes into doing chores for them while the victims are happily unaware that they are being used. The same is true with generosity. "He who pays the fiddler calls the tune" is a common saying among the well-off.

Elite people are well-educated and speak excellent English. Ingrained are the proper uses of lie/lay, who/whom, from/than, et cetera. Obvious grammatical errors are red flags. Yet nothing is easy with these people. English that is painfully correct is considered affected, as are fancy words or French and Italian phrases. And another misstep is a plumy-voiced accent: it's "too-MAY-tohs," not "tah-MAH-tahs." When choosing words, Old Money uses the plainest: draperies are curtains, yachts are boats, and goblets are glasses. While the list is endless, bluntness underlies word preferences.

Table One is a list of New Money / Old Money translations.

Table One: A Brief Lexicon

New Money Says:	Old Money Says:
wealthy	well-to-do
rich	well-off
millionaire	very well-off
multimillionaire	loaded
billionaire	stink-o
middle-class	ordinary
fancy	tacky
mansion	house
historic property	big dump
servants	help
Rolls Royce	car
valuable	worth owning
antiques	good things
heirloom	hand-me-down
perfection	not bad
Aw, shit!	Oh, shit!

CHAPTER SEVEN: THE GRAND OLD MAN

The Skeleton in the Closet of Old Money

Better to be an ancestor than to have them.

—Sigmund Freud

Everybody has some interest in forebears even if going back no further than his or her grandparents. Times past are a subject for occasional consideration, although they hardly pervade the day-to-day. For Old Money, history is ever present. While regular people assume famous ancestors are a source of pride, for rich old families ancestors are a source of dread. The wellspring of their wealth is frequently a font of embarrassment. Peering down upon every historic family is the "grand old man." He was the fortune founder, the ark builder, and the one from whom all blessing flowed. His reputed daring, heroism, and sagacity are told and retold. In moments of confidentiality plutocrats admit to each other that they really know very little about this guy. And what is known ain't pretty.

All grand-old-man stories are the same and none bear critical thinking. The plotlines are always poor boys rising to wealth through uncanny smarts and pluck. Still, there are never logical explanations for these magical transformations; significant parts of rags-to-riches tales are missing. How one of my great-grandfathers morphed from orphan into lumber baron, or at least lumber baronet, is a mystery. Likewise, the patriarch of my wife's family inexplicably rose from an Illinois hamlet to become a cohort of Henry Flagler. Such blanks make descendants uneasy. While not every American fortune is based on something criminal, most are based on something fishy.

In our sanitized twenty-first century we assume that fortunes are made in tall buildings with sealed windows. The machinery of wealth is now a computer, and a mogul is the master or mistress of point-and-click derring-do. This was not true of Old Money fortunes. Great wealth was made in ugly places by grubby, rapacious people.[46] Looking into the past too deeply can be disconcerting. Many gracious Yankee families are rooted in the slave trade.[47] And branches of the Forbes clan shipped opium between India and China, the nineteenth-century equivalent of Columbian drug lords.[48] Scions carry a contradictory mix of admiration and revulsion toward their forefathers.[49] This puts Old Money men in a double bind: they both must, and must not, be like the grand old man. Woe to the male who carries a famous name. On one hand he is scoffed at for not having the chops of his ancestor. Yet had he the mendacity of his progenitor he would become a social outcast. Some boomers did attempt swashbuckling in the style of the grand old man, yet tried to do so as gentlemen. The results were usually disastrous. One example is Edgar Bronfman, Jr., born in 1954. He made a huge splash when he sold off billions in DuPont stock owned by his family's liquor company, Seagram's. That money went into a glittering entertainment conglomerate that foundered. The legendary Seagram & Sons faded away.[50]

I was raised on tales of grand old men. And how weary were my parents of reminding me that I was not living up to that glory. That no kid born in 1951 had much chance of distinguishing himself in the War of 1812 was beside the point. My ancestors were looking down and scowling. Nobody wins with scowling ancestors: if I did nothing I was a wuss, and if I did something I was a damned fool. Today I realize that my ancestry is a tangle of fact, surmise, and bullshit. The hard information I have about the Crusader, the Pilgrim, the Commodores, and the Civil War general would hardly fill a Post-it note. And with the aid of the Internet, I have happened upon some tidbits that I wish I didn't know.

My Southern gent father-in-law had no interest in my

New England ancestors. His people came to St. Augustine decades before the Pilgrims stumbled ashore. Nonetheless, the facts about the grand old men in his family are just as jumbled as my own. My wife has many disjointed scraps of information about the Savannah Baldwins, Powells, Fontaines, and Porters with confusing family trees, tattered letters, and unsorted photos. She has often mentioned having a certified genealogist sort this out. She wants the whole story.

Maybe it would be best if we left well enough alone.

CHAPTER EIGHT: A HOUSE TOUR

The Simple Life of Old Money

Upon entering, you behold a world of graceful charm and incomparable taste.

—Sales pitch, www.realtor.com

A*n appraiser must notice everything. That is my job. The particular position of the talon on a claw-and-ball table indicates a Charleston, Newport, or Philadelphia origin. An experienced appraiser can tell sterling silver from plate by smell. A shadow that fails to fall correctly separates a copyist's painting from a master's. It is all a matter of nuance. Without entirely re-alizing it I was always observing the nuances of my Old Money clients as I valued their collections. They were masters of subtlety and misdirection. Their easy manners, blunt speech, and plain clothing were natural and unaffected, yet at the same time set* *them apart. To be noticeably unnoticeable was their goal. Within a single room may well have been a dozen heart-stopping treasures even as the overall effect was completely modest.*

Take, for example, a household I inspected outside of Philadelphia. To the casual viewer it was a pretty stone farmhouse and nothing grand. There were no gates, fountains, or formal gardens. A gravel drive led past lumpy, stinky bushes to a simple entrance. The front hall was dark and low. The kitchen was to the left and a study to the right. Straight ahead was a sitting room with the dining room behind it. The only obvious luxury was a pretty greenhouse. Otherwise the overall effect was merely pleasant.

The sitting room was smallish and bright. It had yellow walls, white woodwork, and pale rugs. A mantle centered on one wall was opposite a French door opening to the backyard. The slipcovered chairs looked comfortable. Clusters of little bibelots topped tables and a big trophy sat in one corner. Two horse paintings hung above the sofa. The dining room had traditional mahogany furniture. A portrait dominated this room with a huge tea set placed beneath it. The kitchen was as plain as dry toast. It had white cupboards, linoleum countertops, and cork floors. The only small appliance in sight was a toaster. The study had a fireplace, twin leather chairs, old tables, and a couple landscapes. It was a handsome and well-situated house, even if surprisingly ho-hum for the heiress to a huge fortune. At least that is as it would have seemed to an outsider.

Someone in the know appreciated that the farmhouse sat on

many acres in a particularly desirable part of Bucks County. The casually untended land was worth several million were it broken into house lots; absolute privacy had a price. Of course there were no gates or fountains; they would draw unwanted attention from the road. The lumpy bushes were specimen English yews. Squinting in the dark front hall, I spotted a Chester County tall clock that Winterthur would do backflips to own. The sitting room was a wonder of understatement. The two horse paintings were by George Stubbs, each worth an Upper East Side town house. Those pretty tables bore the stamp of Martin Carlin, furniture maker to Marie Antoinette. Clutches of spinach jades and enamel boxes covered the tables, even the tiniest worth five figures. The pictures of children here and there were not the usual photos, rather watercolors by Madame Shoumatoff. That horse racing trophy was thirty-six inches high, solid gold, and presented to my client's grandfather by King George V. Somehow even this jaw-dropping cup was not imposing and only hummed softly from its perch.

As an art lover I knew the dining room portrait was a major Thomas Eakins. The Tiffany tea set was so massive that the houseman had to help me haul it to the horse scales for weighing. John Constable painted the landscapes in the study, and a Fragonard hung in a side hall. The entire house was chockablock with one marvel after another. Nevertheless, every item revealed itself quietly and nothing commanded attention so much as merely suggesting that it might be worth looking upon.

The owners were just as unassuming. She was a polite wom-

an with short, dark hair, wearing a sweater set, tweed skirt, and flat shoes. Her only jewelry was a square diamond engagement ring of no more than two or three carats. She was agreeable and at the same time not chatty; any discussion as to the dollar value of her possessions would have been ill-mannered. It was her duty to telegraph that money meant nothing to her. The husband was more talkative and gave me background information helpful for the appraisal. He had no bluff or bluster. Once when I mentioned that some porcelain seemed mended he divulged that his mother-in-law threw things. Tiny windows can reveal broad vistas.

My relationships with clients rarely became social. I was in their houses on business; we did not stay in touch. I do know that these bastions of the old guard died in the late 1980s. The fate of their property is unknown to me. I cannot say that all my inventories were so noteworthy. Certainly I was in rarified air while I worked within that farmhouse, but I had many remarkable clients with extraordinary houses. I fear that I took it all for granted. I assumed that there would always be quiet people with easy manners, living unpretentiously amid wonderful things.

Oh, I was so wrong.

CHAPTER NINE: CLOTHING MATTERS

The Gear and Garb of Old Money

*A sense of being perfectly well dressed gives a feeling of
inward tranquility that religion is powerless to bestow.*

—Overheard by Ralph Waldo Emerson
and noted in his journal

In the eighteenth century, men wore breeches with stockings. It was a flamboyant age and gentlemen were often clad in embroidered satin. The Quakers would have none of that. To separate themselves, Quaker men wore suits of plain gray. It was a statement of simple taste and moral superiority. By the 1820s breeches were universally replaced with long pants, although a few Philadelphia Quakers continued wearing gray breeches into the 1890s. It was an ostentatious display of how unostentatious Quakers considered themselves.[51]

Of course that was laughable. Nonetheless, the Old Money crowd does have clothing issues. Like those Quakers they also assert their superiority by bucking fashion trends. Distrusting new styles, established wealth overcompensates with dull and tatty garments. Among the bon ton a whiff of shabby is the perfume of aristocracy. Wearing no socks implies that a man has just come from boating; frayed collars connote a casual disregard for middle-class standards. Do not be fooled: appearing down at the heels is a studied affectation. Prince Philip, for one, is a master.

Long ago only the ruling class had noticeably good clothing, and rank was determined by a glance. And the rich dressed richly indeed. Old photos show them so heavily swathed in velvets, brocades, and tassels that their getups seem made by crazed upholsterers.[52] Then the Industrial Revolution put stylish garments within reach of ordinary buyers. While speech and manners may well still signal someone's station, clothes became less certain.

As new money adopted fancier attire, Old Money abandoned brocade gowns and golden watch chains. To be anti-chic became chic, a perfect Old Money conundrum. They chose to hide in plain view with wardrobes that were classically styled yet unobtrusive. Tiny details became significant; the perfect-nothing handbag or deceptively plain wristwatch indicated preeminence. If one saw, one knew. If one did not know, one did not have to see. Saks Fifth Avenue, Neiman Marcus, and Bonwit Teller were reliable standbys; bespoke duds were purchased on Savile Row in London. Owning Louis Vuitton trunks required a trip to Paris, and Gucci togs meant a stop in Rome. Drip-dry, polyester, and vinyl were left to lesser mortals.

Those lesser mortals kept nipping at Old Money's heels. In the early 1980s two phenomena arose: conglomerates and a guy from the sticks named Ralph Reuben Lifshitz. These two forces seriously eroded genteel garb as a class signifier. After the 1970s recession, carriage trade shops struggled. Some stores dear to good taste closed, such as Peck & Peck. Even Lilly Pulitzer retired. To survive, many brands sold out to conglomerates. The new owners all hit upon one solution: cheapen the goods and mass-market them. Hardy Amies merged with a department store. Gucci, Burberry, and Vuitton products were made available to middle-class shoppers. Even Cartier plunked a store in a Florida mall across from a GapKids. And when every luxury brand went on line, exclusivity was kaput.

Patricians faced another assault. Mr. Lifshitz, otherwise known as Ralph Lauren, flooded America with his ersatz vision of lordly living, an aristocracy of fake peacocks screeching on fake lawns.[53] To the truly privileged the entire Ralph Lauren concept was tin-plated, lacking context and nuance. Regardless, Ralph Lauren was a marketing genius and the public chose aspiration over authenticity. By pulling on a Polo brand jockstrap any guy could be a toff. Old Money faced a crisis: their old style was now a new style and new styles were dreaded. For the first time the establishment was self-conscious about tweeds and button-down shirts, afraid of being taken for Ralph Lauren wannabes. Everything preppy became a joke.[54] Traditionalists retreated to neutral, common-denominator garments and disposable accessories. Now those of the first water choose outfits with no cultural or sartorial impact at all. The exquisite understatement of old guard raiment is gone. Today, even knowing eyes see nothing.

The I-generation looks upon their grandparents' clothes as no less ridiculous than Louis XIV's. Finding their roots a mixture of confusion and embarrassment, well-off I-gens joined the Levi-clad masses. If the goal of Old Money is to draw no attention, it has triumphed. Old Money has gone from unassuming to downright imperceptible.

Figure 4: Good-bye To All That

CHAPTER TEN: GOOD-BYE TO ALL THAT

The Sunset of Old Money

The history of the world ... is the history of fallen aristocracies.

—Professor Joseph Epstein, University of Chicago

G randmother Porter had a big silver tea set, a real hum-dinger. My wife had eyed that tea set since childhood and eventually it became hers. After a lifetime of anticipation she triumphantly placed it in our dining room. There it sat in splendor for about a week. Then we put it in the garage.

That tea set is a painfully obvious metaphor for Old Money America. Both are a contradictory mélange of substantial worth and questionable utility: too good to junk but too peculiar to keep. We are trying to pass the silver and its history on to future generations. So far we have failed. The kids in the family have no more interest in that tea set and the baggage that comes with *it than in hoopskirts and lace mitts. It is little wonder that young people have no regard for traditions. The highest echelon has failed to retain its place in modern society and exert any influence on contemporary life.*

While no one wants the nabobs to be society's dominant voice, that we have no voice is equally absurd. The upper class failed not only to lead, it failed to even participate. The gentry fell short of instilling its highest ideals into our current civilization. Americans still crave human dignity, civility, and personal understatement. While manners and optimism are collapsing, Old Money is silent. Reliable old-school voices, such as William F. Buckley and Dominick Dunne, have died; Tom Wolfe is lately unreliable. The few that do come forward muck up their message with politics, thus making fools of themselves. That Paris Hilton is the face of Old Money in America is nobody's fault except Old Money's.

In the age of Obama, Old Money is no longer the preeminent anything anymore. Class in America is determined solely by income. Education, culture, and historical perspective mean little now. This income-only standard puts Lindsay Lohan in the aristocracy and ranks not-rich Lees and Roosevelts as equal to bums. No longer do once-renowned names elicit popular interest. That so few Americans care anymore is the real stake through the heart of Old Money. Our country has moved on and tossed away the greatest jewel from the Old Money crown: prestige.

The old identifiers of the lofty life are today's detritus. This discourages the Brahmans' will to soldier on. Like any ethnic group or subculture that sees its world passing away, Old Money is in mourning. Many landmarks both physical and psychological are vanishing. Personally, one example is my grandfather's demesne. Eight little houses now stand in his meadow, and garages occupy what was the rose garden. Once all crisp clapboards and green shutters, Grampy's colonial is now an eyesore. It was right that my father did not sacrifice his career to keep the old place afloat. Still ...

Old Money's stuff has nowhere to go. There are more antique doohickeys and gilded widgets than homes that want them. Every day the chattels of old families are auctioned off all across America. Prices drop as demand shrinks and items once indispensable to fancy living go begging. When I tell my granddaughter that everything I own will be hers, horror flickers over her face. I am thinking heritage. She is thinking garage sale. She will inherit our high-end junk because my wife and I are too steeped in nostalgia to ditch it.

My wife and I know that more than formal houses and impractical furnishings are finished. We understand that we exist in the post-sunset of Old Money America. Our wealth has eroded, we have little assurance about anything anymore, and that we possess any prestige is laughable. Even though we live modestly by standards of the past, our habits are becoming archaic. Old Money Americans have become curios, rather like the Amish. For my down-to-earth nephews, a visit to my house is like a trip to a theme park. Thank goodness they are too polite *to laugh out loud at my fuddy-duddy suits and quaint preoccupations.*

I can only quote them the words of their Great-grandfather Benson: "Money isn't everything. But gosh, it's so convenient!"

APPENDIX

Does Lester Lanin play in the windmills of your mind? Have you had your picture in *Town & Country*? Do you consider peanuts hors d'oeuvres? Is changing to summer slipcovers a kick? Are you just so over riding English saddle? Can you pronounce "Cholmondeley"?

Table Two is a checklist of Old Money minutiae and fixations. Be warned: if you can respond to 80 percent of the questions you are in danger of being Old Money.

Table Two: An Old Money Checklist

FAMILY FALDEROL	• Can you name all your great-grandparents by order of birth? • Does your old family place now charge admission? • Did you get Dad's Calatrava, but alas, not Grandma's Candela? • Do you check the index of history books for your clan moniker? • Does any male relation have III, IV, or V after his name?
FINANCIAL STUFF	• Do you know how much cash you have on you at any time? • Why does "clipping coupons" not mean cents off on Dulcolax? • Can you explain why it is pointless to try breaking a trust fund? • Did your grandmother have a foundation, and no, it did not lace up the back? • Are you down to your last million? Is it hell?
SCHOOL DAYS	• Does the whole Ivy League thing bore you terribly? • You do know the difference between Penn and Penn State, right? • Did you take art history? • Were you nice to the townies? • Was *A Separate Peace* required reading?

HEARTH AND HOME	• Do you have more table linens than toilet paper? • Can you explain how "claw and ball" is not a venereal disease? • Does eating in the kitchen depress you? • Did you get your mother's case of blue Fitzhugh? • Is there a silver-plated windshield in your pantry?
TRIMMING YOUR JIB	• Just for kicks, do you sometimes wear an ascot? • Are you rejoicing that Lily Pulitzer is back? • Do you debate with yourself if Belgian shoes are sissy? • Is frayed better than new? • Would you rather have a viper in your pocket than a comb?
MATTERS AUTOMOTIVE	• Do you realize that a "Silver Ghost" is not a Halloween costume? • Does your garage have a pagoda top? • Is a rusty Volvo one sweet ride? • Are new mufflers bourgeois? • Would you rather crawl than arrive in a limousine?

MR. SPORTY	• When looking at horses, do you just see vet bills? • Do you love standard apricots? • Would you pay forty grand for a Crowell? Four hundred grand for a Hinckley? • Can you explain how an "over and under" is not a sex position? • Do you actually consider bird watching a sport?
M'LADY OF THE MANOR	• Do you have reticulated ramekins? • Can you believe how tacky the curtains are in the White House? • Are you always coming across diamonds you've forgotten about? • Do you thank God each and every day for sweater sets? • (Sotto voce) "Which Forbes is he?"

Table Three is a list of recommended fiction for further Old Money studies.

Table Three: Recommended Fiction

Auchincloss, Louis, *The Rector of Justin*
Balzac, Honoré de, *Cousin Pons* and *Lost Illusions*
Collins, Wilkie, *Basil*
Dickens, Charles, *Bleak House*
Dunne, Dominick, *The Two Mrs. Grenvilles*
Fitzgerald, F. Scott, *The Great Gatsby*
Galsworthy, John, *The Forsyte Saga*
James, Henry, *The Spoils of Poynton*
Marquand, J. P., *Wickford Point* and *So Little Time*
Maugham, W. Somerset, *The Razor's Edge*
O'Hara, John, *Ten North Frederick* and *From the Terrace*
Sinclair, Upton, *Oil!*
Steinbeck, John, *The Winter of Our Discontent*
Waugh, Evelyn, *A Handful of Dust*
Wharton, Edith, *The House of Mirth*
Whitehead, Colson, *Sag Harbor*

Table Four is recommended nonfiction that informed *Old Money America*, even though it is not directly referenced in the text. See "Endnotes" for bibliographic material.

Table Four: Recommended Nonfiction

Aimes, Hardy, *The Englishman's Suit*, Quartet Books, 1994.

Amory, Cleveland, *The Proper Bostonians*, Dutton, 1947.

Amory, Cleveland, *The Last Resorts*, Harper & Brothers, 1952.

Baldwin, William, *Billy Baldwin Remembers*, Harcourt, Brace Jovanovich, 1974.

Baltzell, E. Digby, *Sporting Gentlemen: Men's Tennis from the Age of Honor to the Cult of the Superstar*, The Free Press, 1995.

Collier, Peter, *The Rockefellers: an American Dynasty*, Holt McDougal, 1976.

Epstein, Joseph, *Snobbery, the American Version*, Houghton Mifflin Company, 2002.

Gross, Michael, *740 Park: The Story of the World's Richest Apartment Building*, Broadway Books, 2005.

McCullough, David, *Mornings on Horseback*, Simon & Schuster, 1981.

Post, Emily, *Etiquette*, Funk & Wagnall's, 1922.

Tuchman, Barbara, *The March of Folly*, Alfred A. Knopf, 1984.

Winokur, John, editor, *The Rich Are Different*, Random House, 1996.

Table Five: Specialist Libraries and Institutions

The author would like to acknowledge these fine institutions for their invaluable information and inspiration toward the creation of this book.

Forbes House Museum, Milton, MA
Historic Savannah Foundation
Peabody Essex Museum
Pennsylvania Society of the Sons of the Revolution
The Athenaeum of Philadelphia
The Boston Athenaeum
The Charlestown Foundation
The Henry Charles Lee Room of the Van Pelt Library, University of Pennsylvania
The Mayflower Society
The Museum of the City of New York
The New York Society Library
The Redwood Library and Athenaeum, Newport, RI
The Wadsworth Athenaeum, Hartford, CT

ABOUT THE AUTHOR

John Hazard Forbes is a *Mayflower* descendant and an Ivy League graduate. The Hazards were the richest family in colonial Newport. The Forbes are listed in *Burke's Peerage*. His wife is a Powell of Savannah.

Outside his immediate circle, his thirty-five-year career as an art expert and appraiser gave him unusual entrée into the houses and lives of the old rich. Art experts must be observant; even the smallest detail cannot be overlooked. So along with their collections John Hazard Forbes closely examined the customs, manners, and viewpoints of America's upper crust.

He offers an insider's perspective. Everything in *Old Money America* is based on his interactions with these remarkable, if often peculiar, people. Having known the elites of New York, Pennsylvania, the Midwest, New England, and the South, John Hazard Forbes is in a unique position to observe and report on Old Money in America.

ABOUT THE ILLUSTRATOR

Audrey Heffner-Villegas is a leading Florida artist-illustrator, with a studio in Naples. Her creation, CHARLES HOMER BIRD, enlivens the pages of this book. Audrey lives on a small farm with her husband and son amid a menagerie of exotic birds and orchids.

ABOUT THE EDITORS

Pamela Goett is a veteran book and magazine editor. She splits her time between Manhattan and the former one-room schoolhouse she has restored in Malden Bridge, New York. Pam was the first person I ran the idea of this book by; her enthusiasm and encouragement are greatly appreciated.

Many thanks to Sarah Disbrow of iUniverse. She refused to tolerate my slippy-sloppy first draft and made me up my game. Thank you, Sarah!

ENDNOTES

AN INTRODUCTION TO OLD MONEY

1. An elite subculture of rich black Americans arose in the eighteenth century. In 1860, the real and personal wealth of free blacks was placed at $50,000,000.
   See Birminghan, Stephen, *Certain People, America's Black Elite*, Little Brown and Company, 1977, pp. 89–92.

2. Sullivan, Paul, "Wealth Matters: Too Rich to Worry? Not in This Downturn," *The New York Times*, Oct. 3, 2009.

3. Marjorie Merriweather Post was a Battle Creek girl. Like all the cereal heirs, she swept up her riches and left town.
   See Rubin, Nancy, *American Empress: The Life and Times of Marjorie Merriweather Post*, Villard Books, 1995.

4. WASP ("White Anglo-Saxon Protestant") is a punchy yet slippery term. Technically, the author is a WSIP, white Scots-Irish Protestant, married to a WASC, white Anglo-Saxon Catholic.

5. Beebe, Lucius, *The Big Spenders*, Doubleday & Co. Inc., 1966.

6. Baltzell, E. Digby, *The Philadelphia Gentleman: The Making of a National Upper Class*, The Free Press, 1958.

7. Nelson Aldrich, Jr., argues that stereotypes of the vapid rich are un-fair and based on political and media-biased constructs. The author has known too many rich twits to be quite so generous.
See Aldrich, Nelson, Jr., *Old Money, The Mythology of Wealth in America*, Allworth Press, 1996, pp. 106–140.

CHAPTER ONE: '37 PACKARD

8. Most of Caroline Hazard's Browning material is now in the Arm-strong Browning Library at Baylor University.

CHAPTER TWO: HIDING IN PLAIN SIGHT

9. Josephson, Matthew, *Robber Barons: The Great American Capitalists*, Harcourt Brace, 1934.

10. See Baltzell, E. Digby, *The Protestant Establishment, Aristocracy & Caste in America*, Vintage Books, 1964.

11. In the first week of January 1958, the Dow Jones Industrial Average was 499. Exactly fifty years later, the DOW was 12,800.
See the NYSE.TV Web site.

12. Royal Barry Wills was a much admired architect of the post-WWII era. In his book, *Houses for Homemakers*, he estimated the construc-tion cost of a fifteen-room colonial mansion with servants' wing and three-car garage at $42,300.
See Wills, Royal Barry, *Houses for Homemakers*, E. M. Hale & Com-pany, 1945, p. 82.
Hubbard Cobb's *Your Dream Home: How to Build It for Less than $3,500* was a popular book in the 1950s. In it Cobb included designs for pretty stone Tudors with material costs at about $3,250 each.
See Cobb, Hubbard, *Your Dream Home: How to Build It for Less than $3,500*, H.M. Wise & Co., 1950, pp. 455–496.

13. Reitlinger, Gerard, *The Economics of Taste*, Hacker Art Books, 1982, vol. II.
The Smithsonian Archives of American Art has a collection of American art auction catalogs from 1785 to 1962.

14. In 1959, a top-of-the line Mercedes-Benz 220SE was $9,000.

15. When the author's sister graduated from Wellesley in the mid-1960s, the entire cost for her four years was about $12,000. In 2009, four years at Wellesley is $200,000.

16. In 1954, the author's father was hired by the Kellogg Company as an engineer. At best, his experience and education were shaky. He later became vice president of research and development.

17. Persico, Joseph E., *The Imperial Rockefeller: A Biography of Nelson A. Rockefeller*, Simon & Schuster, 1982.

18. Aarons, Slim, *Once Upon a Time*, Abrams, 2003, p. 67.

19. Armory, Cleveland, *Who Killed Society?*, Harper & Brothers, 1962.

20. Biographies of John F. Kennedy, Jr., tend to be so gushing that a balanced assessment of his life may yet to be written.
    See Blow, Richard, *American Son: A Portrait of John F. Kennedy, Jr.*, Henry Holt & Co., 2002.

21. Lewis, Michael, *Liar's Poker*, W.W. Norton & Co., 1989.

22. Biographies of George W. Bush tend to be so vitriolic that a balanced assessment of his life may yet to be written.
    See Minutaglio, Bill, *First Son: George W. Bush and the Bush Family Dynasty*, Three Rivers Press, 2001 edition.

23. Caroline Kennedy's wayward attempts to secure the seat of Senator Clinton also diminished notions about aristocrats as born leaders.
    See Confessore, Nicholas & Hakim, Danny, "Kennedy Drops Bid for Senate Seat, Citing Personal Reasons," *The New York Times*, January 21, 2009.

24. Brookhiser, Richard, *The Way of the WASP: How It Made America, and How It Can Save It, So to Speak*, Maxwell Macmillan, 1991.

25. Baltzell, *op. cit.*, pp. 75–76.

CHAPTER THREE: HUSH, MONEY

26. *Now, Voyager* has a will-reading scene. This 1942 Warner Brothers film can be viewed in its entirety on the Web.
    See GOOGLE.com / Video / "Now, Voyager."

CHAPTER FOUR:
THE IVY CHARITY GALA REGISTER

27. The author was a board member of a New York charity benefiting disabled persons. Ashamed as I am to admit it, "No crips!" was a mantra at special event planning sessions.

28. The *Social Register* is published annually by the Social Register Association, 28 West 23rd St., New York, NY.

29. Oddly, "The" was never part of its title.

30. As early as 1962, the exclusivity of the *Social Register* was in serious doubt.
See "Society: Open End," *TIME* magazine, July 20, 1962.

31. Burke's Peerage Partnership, *Burke's Peerage & Gentry*, 2008.

32. Social Register Association, *Social Register*, New York. 1887.

CHAPTER FIVE: NUTHATCH LANE

33. Maysles, Albert and Maysles, David, *Grey Gardens / the Beales of Grey Gardens*, DVD, Criterion Collection, 2001.

34. Sheldon, George William, *Artistic Houses*, Appleton & Co., 1883.

35. See Reitlinger, Gerard, *op cit.*, Vol. I.

36. James, Henry, *The American Scene*, Harper & Brothers, 1908, pp. 216–217.

37. Lopate, Philip, *John Koch: Painting a New York Life*, Scala Publishers, 2001.
The following Web page includes the evocative 1950 "Family Group," the 1956 "Cocktail Party" and the 1971 "Morning."
See GOOGLE / John Koch/ Search Images.

38. Burden, Shirley, *The Vanderbilts in My Life: A Memoir*, Ticknor & Fields, 1981, p. 127.

39. This layering, or rather the lack of it, is the problem with boring historic houses and lifeless period rooms. Curators determine a specific

period and no items dating from before or after are allowed, nor is the stuff of everyday living. This makes for arid set pieces.

Two historic houses are layered with generations of family accumulations: "Kingscote" in Newport and "Tudor Place" in Georgetown. Both give the impression of still being inhabited.

See hhp://lcweb2.loc.gov/pp/ "Historic American Building Survey" / Tudor Place, #5.hh.

Ibid., /Kingscote, #1.hh.

40. Graham, Lawrence Otis, *Our Kind of People: Inside America's Black Upper Class*, Harper Collins, 1999, chapter VIII.

41. Meyer, Eugene L., "A Welcoming Enclave with Roots in a Snub," *The New York Times*, September 3, 2009.

42. Vanderbilt, Arthur T., II, *Fortune's Children: The Fall of the House of Vanderbilt*, William Morrow, p. 413.

43. Benjamin Bradlee, former editor of *The Washington Post*, and his wife, Sally Quinn, have invested twenty-three years into restoring Grey Gardens. As one example of how badly the house had deteriorated, Ms. Quinn chanced to touch the keys of a dilapidated grand piano. The piano collapsed and fell through the floor.

See Scelfo, Julie, "Reinventing Grey Gardens: A Drawn-Out Drama in Itself," *The New York Times*, April 15, 2009.

CHAPTER SIX: OLD MONEY SPEECH

44. The source information on this program came from Alfred Ulmer, Jr., a relation of the author's father-in-law. "Buddy" Ulmer served during WWII in naval intelligence, moved to the OSS, and became a career officer in the CIA.

See Smith, Richard Harris, *OSS: The Secret History of America's First Central Intelligence Agency*, Lyons Press, 1972, p. 205.

45. Many fortune founders were Freemasons. Lodge culture and Old Money culture share characteristics: each group demands decorum among those within the ranks, and both groups maintain auras of secret knowledge. The author is a Freemason.

See Denslow, William R., *10,000 Famous Masons*, 4 vols. 1957–1961.

CHAPTER SEVEN: THE GRAND OLD MAN

46. The ugliness of fortune-making was a theme in Upton Sinclair novels, especially Oil!, written in 1927

47. The Watson Institute for International Studies, *A Forgotten History: The Slave Trade and Slavery in New England*, Brown University @ www.choices.edu.
Rappleye, Charles, *Sons of Providence: The Brown Brothers, the Slave Trade, and the American Revolution*, Simon & Schuster, 2006.
DeWolf, Thomas Norman, *Inheriting the Trade: A Northern Family Confronts Its Legacy as the Largest Slave-Trading Dynasty in U.S. History*, Beacon Press, 2008.

48. The following is verbatim of an original, unpublished document in the author's files:

Canton, February 27th, 1839.

John M. Forbes, Esq.
Boston.

Dear Sir,

We beg leave to inform you that we have resolved to discontinue all connection with the Opium trade in China, and in pursuance of this determination hereby decline any consignment made to us after due time has been allowed for this announcement to reach our friends abroad. Previous consignments we shall of course exert ourselves to the utmost to bring to as favorable a conclusion as the difficulties that surround us will permit.

We remain, Dear Sir,
Your Most Obedient Servants,

RUSSELL & CO.

49. Vanderbilt, Arthur T., II, *Op. cit.*, pp. 1–51.

50. Holdon, Laure M., and Fabrikant, Geraldine, "Shakeup at Vivendi: A Wealthy Family Humbled by Its Own Moves," *The New York Times*, July 3, 2002.

CHAPTER NINE: CLOTHING MATTERS

51. This was told to the author by Dr. Anthony N. B. Garvan, founder and chairman of the American Civilization Department at Penn. "Tony" Garvan (1917–1992) was an unimpeachable source; there was little about old Philadelphia he did not know.
See Sanger, Stephanie, and Snyder, Theresa, "Guide to Anthony Nicholas Brady Garvan," University Archives and Record Center, University of Pennsylvania, December, 1993 @ upenn.edu.

52. Gernsheim, Alison, *Victorian and Edwardian Fashion: A Photographic Survey*, Dover Publications, 1982.

53. Gross, Michael, *Genuine Authentic: The Real Life of Ralph Lauren*, Harper Collins, 2003.

54. *Take Ivy* is cited on sartorial blogs as the Rosetta stone of preppy / Ivy style. In the mid-1960s, a photographer took pictures of students walking about on Ivy League campuses. Despite current commentaries, the clothing depicted had no elitist overtones. The same styles were worn by American males all over the country, including Wally Cleaver on *Leave it to Beaver*.
See Hayshida, T., *Take Ivy*, Fugingahosha, Japan, 1965.

NOTES

NOTES

NOTES

NOTES

NOTES

NOTES

NOTES

NOTES

NOTES

NOTES

NOTES

NOTES

NOTES

CPSIA information can be obtained at www.ICGtesting.com
Printed in the USA
LVOW08s1600250614

391685LV00003B/717/P